How to Use
Child-size Masterpieces
for Art Appreciation

A PARENT AND TEACHER HANDBOOK
ORIGINALLY TITLED *MOMMY IT'S A RENOIR!*

by ALINE D. WOLF

Illustrated by JANINE SGRIGNOLI WOLF

PARENT CHILD PRESS INC
Hollidaysburg PA

For my husband, Jerry, whose extensive art postcard collection was my original inspiration for this project, and for our sons and daughters—

George	Patrick	Christopher
Catherine	Gregory	Dorie
Mary	Charlie	Gina Grace

Parent Child Press Inc.
PO Box 675, Hollidaysburg PA 16648
(866) 727-3682
www.parentchildpress.com

Preface

This handbook, originally titled *Mommy, It's a Renoir!*, is for parents, teachers or any other adults who want to experience the delight of introducing beautiful paintings to young children. It describes a postcard-size art project which my husband and I began informally at home with our own children and which I later adapted for use in pre-school and elementary classrooms.

In more than one way this project departs from the traditional methods of teaching art appreciation. It invites adults who are not necessarily art specialists to present fine art reproductions, in a simple way, to children who have not yet reached the age usually considered appropriate for this subject. And it dispenses with the "Please do not touch" directive which normally accompanies the study of fine art. In all the activities the children handle postcard-size reproductions.

Children as young as three can do the beginning exercises. The succeeding Steps gradually increase in difficulty and are appropriate for each child's level of experience rather than his or her specific age.

I have found that many of these activities are suitable for children with disabilities, particularly for deaf youngsters who find an unusual joy in working with the art cards. In fact, *Child-Size Masterpieces* are appropriate for all ages. Over a long period of time I have shared my collection informally with teen-agers, adults and elderly citizens who enjoyed doing the exercises to test their own knowledge of paintings as well as to meet the work of artists whom they had not previously encountered.

The emphasis in this project is on exposing young children to art reproductions rather than filling them with the facts of art history. Therefore no formal art appreciation courses are necessary for parents and teachers who are presenting *Child-Size Masterpieces* to children. Basic information, such as the title of the painting and the artist's name, are printed on the reverse side of each card. In addition, the Appendix of this manual contains further reference material for readers who desire it.

I particularly want to offer some encouragement to those readers who may hesitate to undertake the project because they feel inadequate in the subject of art. Many years ago when I was answering our own youngsters' questions about the cards, I had to refer constantly to the information printed on the reverse side of the cards. After a relatively short time, however, I was able to recognize the style of many artists; I could guess their names before turning the cards over. "Do you know this one, Mommy?" my children would ask. Sometimes I didn't know and the children seemed comfortable with the fact that I was learning too.

So if you have a gnawing feeling of inferiority whenever art is discussed, don't worry. You will learn in an easy and delightful way, as I did, when you start buying, sorting and sharing *Child-Size Masterpieces* with young children.

A.D.W.
1996

Preface 2006 Edition

Since the 1996 preface was written, there have been some significant changes that have simplified acquiring and preparing the art postcards for this project.

Originally Parent Child Press ordered art postcards from forty different museums around the world, arranged them according to the *Steps* and *Levels* in this hand book and sold them in plastic baggies to be mounted and labeled by the parents and teachers who purchased them. Because art postcards were constantly going out of print, we soon realized that we would have to publish our own books of *Child-Size Masterpieces*. We now have available eight of these books from which art cards can be cut out but no longer require mounting and labeling. In addition we are able to supply small vinyl pocket-folders that do not have to be cut to size and stapled.

Since its inception, this program has put beautiful reproductions of paintings into the hands of young children in many parts of the world, whether they lived on a farm, in a fishing village, in suburbia or in the inner city. In contrast to the many ugly and violent images that are so frequently offered to children, this program enables youngsters to handle child-size masterpieces and absorb their beautiful details. Why shouldn't we give the best to our children?

- A.D.W.

  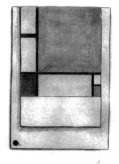

The art cards that appear in this manual are the illustrator's renderings of well-known paintings. The black and white drawings are intended to give you a sense of the original paintings so you can visualize the various exercises that are described. The real art cards which the children will use when doing the exercises are full-color reproductions of the original paintings.

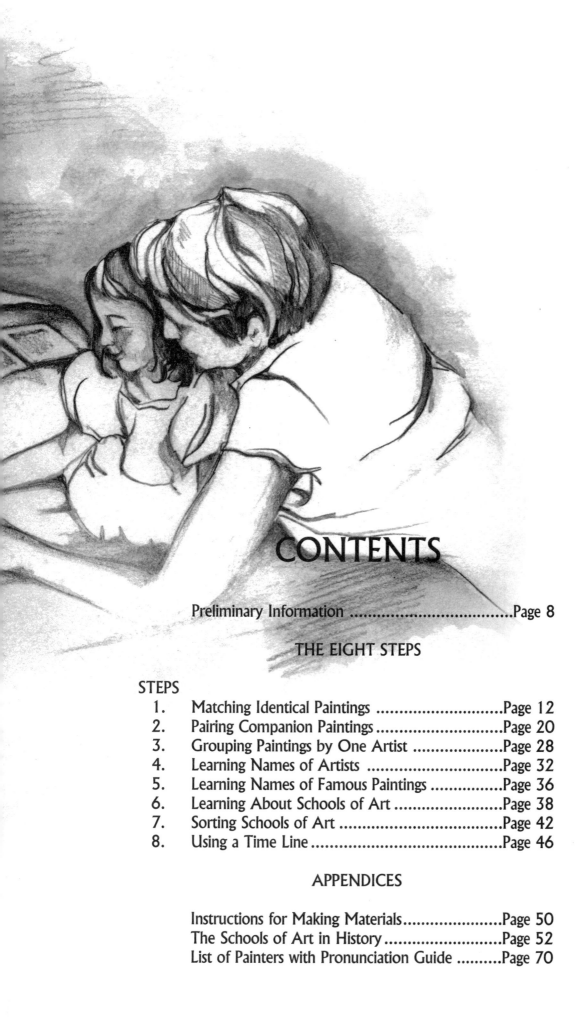

CONTENTS

THE EIGHT STEPS

APPENDICES

Why Use Child Size Masterpieces?

Paintings on the wall are usually not to be handled or moved by children. The same is true of prints in large expensive art books. If adults show such books to youngsters, they usually caution them not to touch, which to the children means not to experience fully. In other words, they are denied the "doing"—their most natural means of reinforcing their visual impressions.

Young children by nature love to use their hands. In fact, when we observe children carefully, we notice that they have an uncontrollable urge to handle everything in sight. They want to pick up and examine each new object they encounter. They are frustrated if placed in an environment of dangerous fragile objects and are constantly told, "Don't touch." This command actively counters one of their strongest natural tendencies.

It seems that information enters children's brains through their hands as often as through their eyes. The renowned educator, Maria Montessori, based her manipulative learning materials on her belief that, "The hand is the chief teacher of the child." Hands not only gather information for children they are the means by which children work through that information, verifying it and reinforcing it.

It is important, therefore, for children to handle some art in their environment. I believe that postcard-size reproductions are ideal for children's activities because they are inexpensive, child-size, lightweight and readily adaptable to many different methods of displaying, comparing, sorting and storing.

Caring for the Child-Size Masterpieces

Permitting young children to handle art cards, however, in no way implies that they should be allowed to abuse them. These reproductions represent some of the greatest treasures of various world cultures and, as such, should be handled with appropriate respect. Although the art cards are not expensive, it is not always convenient, or even possible, to replace them. It is important, then, from the very beginning to show your children how to use the art cards with care.

Your own attitude toward the art cards will be the key to the manner in which the children respect them. Before you introduce the art cards, you might tell the youngsters that in a few days you are going to have a very special project for them. This project will have beautiful pictures painted by famous men and women from many different countries. You will impress the children even more if you let them see that your hands are clean before you handle the art cards. Then ask each child to check her hands before beginning the project. When handling the art cards yourself, do so slowly and deliberately. Shuffling them roughly or stacking them carelessly might indicate to the children that the cards are not really as special as you say they are.

Explaining Reproductions to Children

I always tell the children that each art card is a reproduction of an original painting made by the artist. To insure that the children understand the terms *original* and *reproduction,* I take a child's drawing and say, "You have made an *original.*" Then I use a copy machine to make a reproduction of that original, pointing out that the copy is never as beautiful as the original work of art. I explain that originals are kept in museums where they can be carefully protected. I encourage the children to visit art museums whenever possible.

Programming the Activities for Success

In my experience, children derive the greatest pleasure from art cards if an adult first groups them in particular exercises for the children "to do." Just as a set of blocks of graduated sizes can invite a child to build a tower, a set of *Child-Size Masterpieces,* purposefully pre-selected, can intrigue a child into a delightful learning activity. You, as a parent or teacher, prepare such exercises in advance.

The sequence of the exercises actually promotes success for the child. The first activity—matching three identical pairs of art cards—is so simple it is almost impossible for a child age three or older to fail in doing it. After this initial success, the child is challenged by a new exercise, not too different from the one just mastered, but containing an additional degree of difficulty. The series then continues with a gradually increasing variety of paintings as well as a gradually increasing challenge in the tasks that the child is asked to perform.

Attracting the Child's Interest

Even though I have pre-arranged the order in which you present the *Child-Size Masterpieces,* I suggest that you follow this order in a relaxed, non-structured time-frame. In other words, never pressure a child to do the project. It is not a formal course with lesson plans, deadlines and tests. Rather it is an enrichment project that is most effective when, and if, the child chooses it freely.

The adult's role, therefore, is to intrigue the children, not to force them to work with the art cards. Do this by attractively displaying your art project within the reach of the children and by letting them watch you demonstrate the activities. When you are showing the children how to do the little tasks, do so slowly, at the pace of a child, and rely on your actions more than your words. It is easier for children to imitate the actions they observe than it is for them to translate your verbal instructions into performance.

Attracting children to this project is not difficult. In my experience, whenever a young child first observes an adult or another child using the art cards, the on-looker will nearly always say, "Please, let me do it next!" The project literally sells itself to pre-schoolers.

Child-Size Masterpieces Activities

Following are complete descriptions of eight types of exercises that can be done with *Child-Size Masterpieces*. Each kind of exercise is called a *Step* and some of the *Steps* are sub-divided into graded levels of difficulty. Small pocket-folders are used to hold the art cards for the activities in each *Step*. For easy identification, I have assigned a particular color to the pocket-folders in each of the *Eight Steps*.

All the pocket-folders within each *Step* are the same color and invite the child to do the same kind of task. For example, all the red folders in *Step 1* indicate matching identical paintings. The number of folders in each *step* depends on your budget, the number of children you are working with, and their degree of interest in each of the particular *Steps*.

Step 1 *Matching Identical Paintings—* red folders.
Step 2 *Pairing Two Paintings by the Same Artist—blue folders.*
Step 3 *Grouping Four Paintings by one Artist— green folders.*
Step 4 *Learning the Names of the Artists—* yellow folders.
Step 5 *Learning the Names of Famous Paintings—tan folders.*
Step 6 *Learning about the Schools of Art—gray folders.*
Step 7 *Grouping Paintings from the same School of Art—black folders.*
Step 8 *Using Time Lines of Art—orange folders.*

Buying Child-Size Masterpieces

Some art postcards are sold in the museum shops of nearly every art museum in the United States and abroad. Most museums feature postcard reproductions of their own collections. Only a few include reproductions of paintings from other museums or from private collections. You can, indeed, purchase art cards at museum shops, but in order to get the variety of cards necessary for the *Steps* in this project, you would have to visit a great number of museums.

For your convenience several books of *Child-Size Masterpieces,* featuring full-color reproductions to be cut out and used with the *Steps* in this handbook, have been prepared by the author. Additional art cards are available in sets of the Schools of Art and Time Lines.

For a complete catalog contact:

Parent Child Press Inc.
P.O. Box 675
Hollidaysburg PA 16648
www.parentchildpress.com
866-727-3682

Even if you purchase these basic sets through internet or mail order, you will probably want to augment your collection whenever you visit a museum. It is particularly important to include reproductions from your local museum where the children can view the originals.

There are three points to remember when purchasing art cards for this project:

1. All the cards in these collections are 4 1/2" X 6" or smaller.

2. When purchasing two art cards of the same painting to be used for identical matching, buy them at the same time so they look exactly alike in color intensity and in the proportion of the original painting that is reproduced.

3. While it is always tempting to purchase art cards that are particularly appealing to you, this criterion actually limits the styles in your collection and imposes your taste on the children. A child's preference often differs from that of an adult as well as from that of other children. It seems wiser, therefore, to select cards representing many of the different styles or schools of art recognized in the art world. Descriptions of these schools of art begin on page 52.

Arranging Child-Size Masterpieces in Sets

For many of the exercises described here, the art cards are arranged in sets of six which are to be paired or grouped with other sets of six. For *Steps 1, 2 and 3,* which can be done by children who are not yet able to read, one set is distinguished from another by 1/4" colored dots affixed on the lower left corner of the face of the card. When you prepare your own cards, affix self-stick color-coding labels (available in office supply stores) to the mounting cards. Please note: in the black and white illustrations in this manual

⊕ = a green dot;   ⊜ = a red dot;

◯ = a yellow dot;   ● = a black dot.

Making the Pocket Folders

The most practical storage for two sets of *Child-Size Masterpieces* to be paired is 6" X 8" folder with two pockets inside. Details for making these folders can be found on page 50. Durable vinyl folders are also available from Parent Child Press. Parents doing this project at home may prefer a simpler means of storing their sets, such as using envelopes or clear plastic bags.

Mounting Art Postcards

The reproductions in the books of *Child-Size Masterpieces* are already labeled with the Color-Coded dots or printed labels necessary for this project. However, any additional art cards that you purchase should be mounted on a plain card that will serve as a background for either the dot or label. Complete details for mounting art postcards are on page 50.

Printing Names and Titles

In many of the *Steps,* you will have to print names on mounting cards or titles on folders. Before starting this task, select a simple style of manuscript lettering, such as the one illustrated on page 51, and use this same style throughout the project. When printing the name of an artist, use only the last name or the name by which he or she is most commonly known.

STEP 1

In most pre-school classrooms, children learn to match identical colors, identical shapes, identical pictures of fruit, etc. Because matching identical paintings is simply a variation of these exercises that the children already know how to do, it is the logical first *Step* for this project.

Selecting the Child-Size Masterpieces for Step 1

Careful selection of the art cards for each exercise is vital to the success of this project because the actual selection determines the progression of difficulty. In *Step 1* there are three levels of increasing challenge:

LEVEL 1
EASIEST

All identical pairs in a folder are totally different from all the other pairs in that folder, primarily in subject, but also in color and style. Because of the radical differences between each pair in a folder, it is almost impossible for a child who understands identical matching to do the exercise incorrectly.

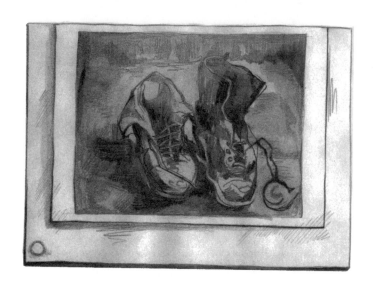

Magritte
First Love
Private Collection

IDENTICAL PAINTINGS

STEP
1

Materials

• At least three, but preferably six or more, red pocket-folders.

• Yellow and green color-coding dots - one package of each.

• Up to six pairs of mounted art cards for each pocket-folder.

Vincent Van Gogh
Boots With Laces
Van Gogh Museum, Amsterdam

Sir James Guthrie
To Pastures New
Aberdeen Art Gallery, Scotland

LEVEL 2
INTERMEDIATE

Some of the identical pairs in each folder are somewhat similar to other pairs in that folder. They can be similar in subject; they can be similar in color *or* they can be similar in style. Because of this slight resemblance between some of the pairs, the child must look more closely at the details in order to make the correct matches.

Pablo Picasso
Le Gourmet
National Gallery of Art,
Washington DC

Using the Names of Artists or Paintings

When introducing Child-Size Masterpieces to very young children, it is not necessary to teach the names of the artists or the names of the paintings. You can mention an artist's name casually whenever you sense that his or her work is a particular favorite of one of the children or whenever the child is using a number of examples of that artist's work. But do not burden youngsters with learning names during these early stages. In the first two *Steps* it is sufficient for the children simply to enjoy looking at and pairing the paintings.

The names of many artists are difficult to pronounce. Before using unfamiliar names with the children, check the pronunciation in the List of Artists on page 70.

John Bradley
Little Girl
National Gallery of Art,
Washington DC

Paul Gauguin
Young Breton With a Goose
Collection Armand Hammer,
Los Angeles

15

LEVEL 3
ADVANCED

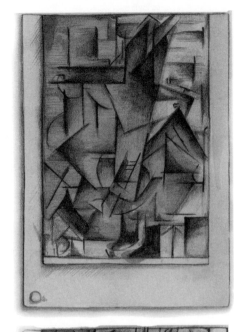

All six identical pairs in each folder are very similar to each other. They are all by the same artist; they all feature the same kind of subject and they are all done in the same style. This high degree of similarity requires the child to check details very carefully in order to do the exercises correctly. Some examples of paintings which can be used in Level 3 folders are listed here:

Six pairs of blue-green garden scenes by Monet.
Six pairs of many-peopled scenes by Breughel.
Six pairs of Cubist paintings by Picasso.
Six pairs of misty seascapes by Turner.
Six pairs of flowers by Redon.

Since all six pairs in each folder in Level 3 are by the same artist, print this artist's name on the front cover of the folder.

Pablo Picasso
Still Life With Liqueur Bottle
The Museum of Modern Art, New York

16

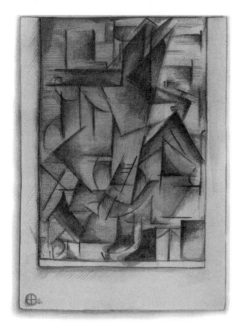

Pablo Picasso
The Guitarist
National Museum
of Modern Art, Paris

Identifying and Storing the Sets for Step 1

1. Place a yellow color-coding dot on the lower left-hand corner of six of the mounting cards, i.e. one card from each of the six pairs you have selected for a folder.

2. Place a green color-coding dot on the lower left-hand corner of each of the remaining six mounting cards.

3. Make sure the cards with the green dots are piled in a different order, top to bottom, from the cards with the yellow dots.

4. Put the cards with the yellow dots in the left pocket of a red folder, and place a yellow dot on this pocket.

5. Put the cards with the green dots in the right pocket of this same folder, and place a green dot on that pocket.

6. Paste a Child-Size Masterpiece on the cover of the completed folder. If possible, this cover card should be identical to, or similar to, one of the cards stored in that folder. At least it should be by one of the same artists.

7. Label each folder as either Level 1, Level 2 or Level 3.

Pablo Picasso
The Violin
Stattsgalerie, Stuttgart

Displaying the Folders

The project is most appealing if the cover cards on each pocket-folder are in full view. There are several alternatives for display, listed in order of preference:

- Lay the folders, face-up, on low slanted shelves, similar to those used to display magazines in libraries.

- Open each folder slightly and stand it upright on a flat shelf. Place several of these upright folders in a row on two or three low shelves.

- Lay the folders face-up in a row on a long, low, flat shelf.

- If your shelf space is very limited, display only a few folders and store the remaining ones in a file sorter or record rack.

Demonstrating Step 1

1. Begin when a child indicates some interest in the folders you have displayed.
2. Sit beside the child at a low table or on the floor. If demonstrating on the floor, use a large plain-colored mat as your working area.
3. Temporarily put aside three of the six pairs from a Level 1 folder and use only the three remaining pairs for your demonstration.
4. Point out to the child that you are handling the cards by grasping only the edges of the cards rather than putting your fingers on the art reproductions.
5. Remove the set of three cards from the left pocket and lay them in a vertical row.
6. Remove the set of three cards from the right pocket and place each one beside its identical mate.
7. Point to the two paintings in each pair and be sure the child notices that they are identical.

8. Pick up the art cards in the first vertical row and slide them into the left pocket of the folder so that the identifying yellow dot on the top card is visible above the pocket. Show the child that this dot matches the dot on the pocket, clearly indicating that this pocket is the storage space for the cards with the yellow dots.

9. Mix up the order of the cards in the other vertical row, so that they will not be in the right order for the next user. This maneuver is important here and in all the succeeding exercises, so exaggerate a bit when your are doing it. Replace this second set in the right pocket.

10. Invite the child to do the exercise.

Responding When a Child Makes an Error

1. Don't comment immediately; give the child an opportunity to correct her own mistake.

2. If she doesn't make the correction herself, point to one of the mismatched pairs and ask, "Does this painting look exactly like that one?"

3. If this question does not lead to a correction, the child may not be ready for this exercise. Wait until the child shows renewed interest and then it try it again.

Gradually Increasing the Challenge

In my experience, the first folder in Level 1 is too simple, rather than too difficult, for most children aged three or older. As soon as a child succeeds with it, he is usually ready and eager for a more challenging activity. You can give him this challenge immediately by putting back, one at a time, the three pairs which you had temporarily set aside from this initial folder. When the child can match all six pairs, give him another Level 1 folder for further practice.

Continue this same sequence for Level 2 and Level 3 as the child is ready.

STEP 2 PAIRING COMPANION PAINTINGS

Step 2 offers children a new and fascinating challenge! In this *Step* they are asked to pair companion paintings—two paintings by the same artist that are *not* identical but are similar in both subject and style. When doing this exercise, the children cannot look for identical details as they did in *Step 1*. Instead they try to recognize a similarity in two examples of a painter's work. This task is much more sophisticated, but it can be made so simple that even four year-olds can do it.

When establishing a pair of companion paintings, *you* must be able to recognize immediately the similarity in style; otherwise this similarity will not be obvious to children. In

other words *don't* study the identifying information on the reverse side of the art cards in order to make up a pair. Instead, select two cards in which you can see a strong resemblance in subject, style and color tones. Then check the reverse side to be sure they are by the same artist.

Many painters, such as Picasso, radically changed their style through the years, so an example of their early work may have nothing in common with a piece from a later period. Take particular care, therefore, to choose two paintings for companion pairs done in the same style, which usually means they are from the same period of an artist's work.

Selecting the Child-Size Masterpieces for Step 2   LEVEL 1 EASIEST

Each companion pair must be made up of two vertical or two horizontal paintings. All the companion pairs in one folder must be radically different from each other, primarily in subject but also in style and color.

For example, in one folder you can have the following selections:

A pair of portraits
A pair of landscapes
A pair of still lifes
A pair of abstracts
A pair of flowers
A pair of animals

Pablo Picasso
Child With A Dove
National Gallery, London

Piet Mondrian
Composition, 1921
Kunstmuseum, Basel

18th Century Chinese
Flowers and Birds
Bibliotheque Nationale, Paris

Pablo Picasso
Le Gourmet
National Gallery of Art,
Washington DC

• At least three, but preferably six or more, blue pocket-folders.

• Red and black color-coding dots— one package of each.

• Up to six companion pairs of mounted art cards for each pocket-folder. Each pair in a folder must be by a different artist.

Piet Mondrian
Composition with Red Blue and Yellow

At this level a child will rely mainly on subject clues to select the two paintings by the same artist. The use of such highly contrasting subjects practically insures his success.

18th Century Chinese
Flowers and Birds
Bibliotheque Nationale, Paris

Beatrix Potter
The Tailor Mouse
Tate Gallery, London

LEVEL 2
INTERMEDIATE

Beginning with this level a companion pair can be made up of two verticals, two horizontals or one vertical and one horizontal. The six pairs in each folder are not so radically different from each other as they were in Level 1. Some of the pairs can have similar subjects but should be highly contrasting in style and color. Other pairs can have the same predominant color but contrasting subject matter.

Many combinations of pairs can be used for Level 2. As you work with the project, your experience will soon tell you which assortment of pairs will be gradually more challenging for the children.

For example, in one folder you can have either of the following combinations:

Two highly contrasting pairs of boats
Two highly contrasting pairs of abstracts
Two highly contrasting pairs of flowers
       or
Three highly contrasting pairs of animals
Three pairs in which the predominant color is the same but the subjects are very different.

Franz Marc *The Gazelle*
Rhode Island School of Design Museum

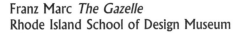

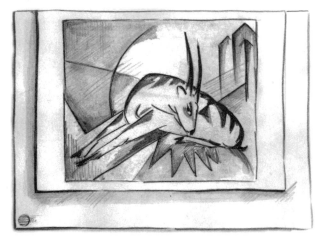

Rembrandt
Lion, Boymans-van
Beuningen Museum

Beatrix Potter
*The Mice Sewing
the Mayor's Coat*
Tate Gallery, London

Since some of the pairs in this level are similar in subject to the other pairs, the child can no longer rely entirely on subject clues when pairing two paintings by the same artist. The color clues are also not so reliable as in Level 1 because two or more pairs in a folder can have the same color tones. Therefore the child begins to look more closely at the style of the paintings when determining a companion pair.

Franz Marc
Sitting Horse

Rembrandt
Elephant
British Museum, London

Pablo Picasso
Pierrot With Flowers

LEVEL 3
ADVANCED

The six pairs in each folder all have the same subject matter. Examples for each of several folders follow:

Six companion pairs of portraits of children

Six companion pairs of abstract paintings

Six companion pairs of paintings of flowers

The key to enabling a child to do this advanced work is a gradual transition from subject clues to style clues. Because the subjects are all the same in Level 3, the child can no longer use subject clues. Colors, too, are frequently similar when the subject matter is similar. So at this point the child must rely on the artist's style to make the correct associations.

Josua Reynolds
The Age of Innocence
Tate Gallery, London

Paul Gauguin
Young Breton With a Bucket
Collection Armand Hammer, Los Angeles

24

Pablo Picasso
The Artist's Son
Picasso Museum, Paris

Preparing the Sets for Step 2

1. Place a red color-coding dot on the lower left-hand corner of six of the mounting cards—i.e. one card from each of the six pairs you have selected for a folder.

2. Place a black color-coding dot on the lower left-hand corner of each of the remaining six mounting cards.

3. Put the cards with the red dots in the left pocket of a blue folder and place a red dot on this pocket.

4. Mix up the order of the cards with the black dots and put them in the right pocket of the same folder. Place a black dot on that pocket.

5. Paste an appropriate Child-Size Masterpiece on every folder cover; label them Level 1, Level 2 or Level 3 and display them as you did for *Step 1.*

Joshua Reynolds
Master Hare
Louvre, Paris

Paul Gauguin
Young Breton With a Goose
Collection Armand Hammer, Los Angeles

Demonstrating Step 2

1. Use a blue Level 1–Easy folder containing only three companion pairs.

2. Tell the child that the exercises in the blue folders are different from those in the red folders. In these new exercises she is not going to pair two paintings that are exactly alike, but two similar paintings by the same artist.

3. Place the first set—the three paintings identified by red dots—in a vertical row.

4. Explain that these paintings were done by three different artists—and each of these artists had a special way that he or she liked to paint. For example, if you are using the geometric abstracts by Mondrian which have square and oblong blocks of color framed by straight heavy black lines, help the child to become aware of this style by asking questions. "Do you think this artist liked to paint people or shapes? Did he like to use bright colors? What kind of lines did he draw around colors?" etc.

5. Select one painting from your second set—the three paintings identified by the black dots—and tell the child you are looking at the style—the special way it was painted.

6. Try it beside each of the three paintings in the first set and tell the child you are looking for a painting in the first set which is painted in this same special style.

7. The child may point to the correct mate in the first set. If not, you make the decision and place it beside its companion.

8. Pair the remaining cards in the second set with their companions in the first set.

9. Point carefully to each pair so the child will notice the similarities.

10. Put the cards back in the pockets and invite the child to do the exercise.

Increasing the Challenge

If you prepare your folders carefully children as young as four will have little or no difficulty in correctly pairing two companion paintings by each of three artists. As soon as a child can do this, add more companion pairs to this initial folder. After he has worked successfully with these, he can try the challenge of Level 2—Intermediate and eventually Level 3—Advanced.

After many years of experience I feel that pairing companion paintings is one of the activities in this project which young children enjoy most. Youngsters age four through eight seem particularly comfortable with the challenge of *Step 2*. They constantly ask for new folders, seeking an ever-increasing variety of paintings to experience.

STEP 3 GROUPING FOUR

Step 3 is an extension of *Step 2*. Instead of pairing only two paintings by each artist, the child is invited to identify and group four paintings by each artist.

Selecting the Child-Size Masterpieces
LEVEL 1
EASIEST

The four paintings by one artist must be similar to each other in both subject and style. At the same time these four paintings must be very different in subject and style from the four paintings by each of the other two artists included in each folder. For example, in one folder you may have the following:

Four paintings of ballet dancers by Degas
Four abstract paintings by Miró
Four paintings by Michelangelo

LEVEL 2
INTERMEDIATE

The subject matter of all the cards in each folder are the same, but the styles of each of the three artists are radically different. Following are examples of three folders of portraits you can have:

Four paintings by Mary Cassatt
Four paintings by Michelangelo
Four paintings by Van Gogh

Four paintings by Renoir
Four paintings by Rembrandt
Four paintings by Rouault

Four paintings by Leonardo da Vinci
Four paintings by Cézanne
Four paintings by Carl Larsson

Edgar Degas
Arabesque
Louvre, Paris

Joan Miró
*Women and Bird
in the Moonlight*
Tate Gallery, London

Michelangelo
Head of Libyan Sibyl

PAINTINGS BY ONE ARTIST

- At least six green pocket folders.

- Yellow, green, red and black color coding dots.

- Four mounted paintings by each of three artists for each double folder.

Edgar Degas
Two Dancers

Ballerina

The Dance With The Bouquet
Louvre, Paris

Joan Miró
Dutch Interior
Museum of Modern Art, NY

Personnages et Chien Devant Le Soleil
Offentliche Kunstsammlung Basel

Woman and Little Girl in Front of the Sun
Hirshhorn Museum Washington DC

Michelangelo
Head of God the Father

Head of Delphic Sibyl

Head of Etruscan Sibyl
Sistine Chapel, Rome

29

LEVEL 3
ADVANCED

All the *Child-Size Masterpieces* in a single folder have the same subject matter and at this level, the styles of the three artists are not so radically different from each other as they were in Level 2. In some cases you can provide this increase in difficulty simply be arranging the art cards you used for Level 2. This new arrangement will require the child to look even more carefully at fine details of style.

For example, you can regroup your three folders of portraits as follows:

Four paintings by Mary Cassatt
Four paintings by Carl Larsson
Four paintings by Renoir

Four paintings by Van Gogh
Four paintings by Cézanne
Four paintings by Rouault

Four paintings by Michelangelo
Four paintings by Rembrandt
Four paintings by Leonardo da Vinci

Preparing the Sets for Step 3

1. Put a yellow dot on the mounting card of one painting by each of the three artists; a green dot on a second painting by each artist; a red dot on the third painting by each artist and a black dot on the fourth painting by each artist.
2. In the space below the painting on each of the mounting cards *in the first set only*—the set with the yellow dots—print the last name of the artist or the name by which he or she is most commonly known. Do not put any names on the remaining three sets.

Preparing the Folders

Since each folder in this *Step* must accommodate four sets of cards, it must be a double one, having four pockets.
1. To make this double folder, attach the back cover of one folder to the front cover of a second folder with either paste, rubber cement or staples.
2. Use a yellow color-coding dot for the first pocket, green for the second, red for the third and black for the fourth.
3. Mix up the sequence of each set and then store each set in the pocket with the corresponding colored dot.
4. Paste an appropriate *Child-Size Masterpiece* on the cover; label as Level 1, Level 2 or Level 3 and display.

Demonstrating Step 3

1. Tell the child that when he uses the green folders he will group four paintings by one artist.
2. Place the first set—the three paintings with the yellow dots—in a vertical row.
3. Remove the second set—green dots—from the folder and place each painting beside its companion in the first set.
4. Remove the third set—red dots—from the folder and place each painting beside its companion in the second set.

5. Remove the fourth set—black dots— and place each painting beside its companion in the third set.

6. When the layout is complete, make sure the child notices that each horizontal row has four paintings by the same artist and each vertical row has three paintings with the same colored dots.

7. Mix up the order of the cards in each vertical row and return them to the appropriate pocket.

8. Invite the child to do the exercise.

Using the Names of the Artists

As you will notice in the illustrations for *Step 3*, each horizontal row of four paintings by one artist is impressive. It will give any child, or even any onlooker, a good idea of the style of that particular artist. Therefore, it is a good time for you to help the child to associate the artist's name with these four examples of his or her work.

I suggested that you print the artist's name on the first set in each folder so that the child can notice it when she is looking at the four paintings by that artist. Even if a child cannot read, she will get a mental picture of the word representing the artist's name. The names are not printed on the other three sets because these four identical names would allow the child to use word clues rather than style clues to form the horizontal rows.

Children can become familiar with the names and works of many important artists in *Step 3* exercises. Add more artists gradually, up to a maximum of six in each folder.

Step 4 is designed for children who can read or are learning to read. It offers them the opportunity to become familiar with the names of many well-known artists by focusing on a particular subject such as "Little Boys" or "Little Girls" and looking at examples of how six different artists treated this subject matter. The children can then learn the names of these six artist's by referring to Control Cards and matching each artist's Name Card to his or her painting.

Selecting the Child-Size Masterpieces

1. There are no separate Levels of difficulty for Step 4. The challenge is approximately the same in each folder.

2. Because Step 4 is specifically designed for learning names, include only paintings by well-known artists, those whose names you will find consistently in art reference books or the "List of Artists" on page 70.

3. The painting or paintings selected for each artist should be representative of the style for which he or she is most commonly known.

4. It is helpful to have some of the major artists represented in several different subject folders so that the children will begin to sense their importance and have repeated practice with their names. For example, paintings by Cézanne could be included under several of the following subjects: Flowers, Still Life, Landscapes, Women, Men, etc.

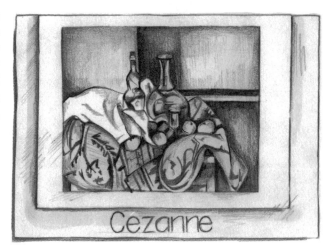

NAMES OF THE ARTISTS

Auguste Renoir
Fruits From the Midi
The Art Institute of Chicago

Materials
• At least three, but preferably six or more small yellow pocket-folders.

• Six 5"x1" labels for each folder made from poster board of the same color and weight as your mounting cards.

• Six duplicate pairs of mounted art cards for each folder. All six pairs feature the same subject matter, each pair by a different artist.

Georges Braque
Still Life With Grapes
The Phillips Collection
Washington DC

Preparing the Sets

1. On one mounting card of each identical pair in a folder, print the name of the artist in the space below the painting. All the cards in this first set are called "Control Cards."

2. Do not print the artists' names on the remaining mounted postcards which are called "Learning Cards."

3. Instead print an exact replica of each artist's name horizontally on a 5" X 1" strip. There will be six of these Name Cards for each folder.

4. Put the Control Cards in the left pocket of each folder.

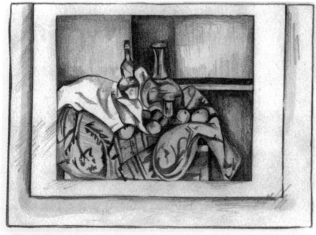

Paul Cézanne
Still Life with Peppermint Bottle
National Gallery of Art Washington DC

5. Put the Learning Cards and the Name Cards in the right pocket of the same folder. Spread out the Name Cards so they will not bulge in the pocket.

6. Paste an appropriate Cover Card on the front of each folder and label it according to the subject. For example: *Paintings of Children With Animals* or *Paintings of Mothers and Children.*

Note: Because the Control Cards are easily distinguished from the Learning Cards; no color-coding dots are necessary for this Step.

Demonstrating Step 4

1. Begin with a folder which contains paintings by some of the artists whose names you introduced in *Step 3.* Thus you can be sure that the child will not be immediately challenged by six "new" names.

2. Remove the Control Cards from the folder and place them in a vertical row saying each artist's name aloud as you handle his or her painting.

3. Explain to the child that the name below each painting is that of the artist who painted it.

4. Remove the Learning Cards from the folder and place each one beside its identical painting.

5. Remove the Name Cards from the folder and select the correct artist's name for each Learning Card by referring to the Control Card. Pronounce each artist's name again and place the Name Card below the painting.

6. When the layout is complete, point out to the child that each pair of paintings and names are identical.

7. Put the cards back in the folder and invite the child to do the exercise. Ask her to pronounce the artists' names as she handles each Control Card and each Name Card.

Increasing the Difficulty

After the child has worked several times with a particular folder, show her how she can challenge herself by reversing the procedure:

1. Remove the materials from the right pocket and place the Learning Cards in a vertical row.

2. Place each artist's Name Card on the appropriate Learning Card while saying each name aloud.

3. Finally remove the Control Cards from the left pocket and place each painting beside its identical mate.

4. Check each Name Card with the Control Card beside it to be sure the names are identical.

5. Move the Name Cards *if* any corrections are necessary.

Follow the Child's Pace

When children are allowed to work in a relaxed atmosphere, they often achieve more than we expect. In my experience youngsters who cannot yet read fluently are sometimes able to do this exercise, apparently using the size and shape of the artist's name and its first letter as a guide. I have watched some of these children succeed; even those who cannot read short words like "does" or "play" can distinguish the name "Rembrandt" from the name "Van Gogh" and place each of these names in its appropriate place. Do not be concerned if a child does not immediately remember the artists' names. If you allow her to proceed at her own pace, she will commit them to memory gradually as she repeats the exercises over a period of weeks or months.

STEP 5 LEARNING THE NAMES

It is neither necessary nor useful for young children to learn all the titles of paintings which they experience in this project. Many titles such as *Composition 1* or *Untitled* are insignificant. Hundreds of paintings are called *Still Life* and hundreds of portraits are known by the names of their subjects—people who may or may not be noteworthy.

Many painters give the same name to several different compositions. Sometimes two or more painters use the same title, such as *The Bridge at Chatou* which was painted by both Van Gogh and Vlaminck. Thus it would only be confusing for children to try to learn the titles of numerous paintings. It is however, worthwhile for them to learn the names of a dozen or more very significant paintings that are widely known by their titles. Children can learn these in an exercise which is similar to *Step 4.*

The Lovers
by Picasso

Selecting the Paintings

There is no hard and fast list of famous paintings. Below is a selection of widely known works from which you can choose six for each folder. Don't hesitate to add others that you feel are significant.

Creation of Adam by Michelangelo
The Night Watch by Rembrandt
Mona Lisa by Leonardo da Vinci
The Last Supper by Leonardo da Vinci
Madonna of the Chair by Raphael
View of Toledo by El Greco
Birth of Venus by Botticelli
The Shrimp Girl by Hogarth
The Age of Innocence by Reynolds
Blue Boy by Gainsborough
Pinkie by Lawrence
Sunday Afternoon on the Island of La Grande Jatte by Seurat

The Swing by Fragonard
A Girl With A Watering Can by Renoir
The Starry Night by Van Gogh
The Lovers by Picasso
Peaceable Kingdom by Hicks
American Gothic by Grant Wood
George Washington by Gilbert Stuart
Arrangement in Black and Gray by Whistler (better known as *Whistler's Mother*)
Broadway Boogie-Woogie by Mondrian
Christina's World by Andrew Wyeth
Persistence of Memory by Salvador Dali

The Age of Innocence
by Reynolds

OF FAMOUS PAINTINGS

Materials
- Two to four tan pocket-folders.
- Six 5"x1" labels of mounting card material for each folder.
- Six identical pairs of famous Child-Size Masterpieces for each folder.

Preparing the Sets and Folders

1. Make Control Cards by printing the name of the painting and the name of the artist (preceded by the word "by") on one mounting card of each identical pair in a folder. Since both names must fit in the space below the painting, use letters smaller than those which you used in *Step 4.*

2. Leave this space blank on each Learning Card.

3. On each of the six Name Cards print the title of one of the paintings, the word "by" and the artist's last name.

4. Put the Control Cards in the left pocket of the folder.

5. Put the Learning Cards and the six labels in the right pocket of the folder.

6. Paste an appropriate Child-Size Masterpiece on the cover of each folder; label them "Famous Paintings #1", "Famous Paintings #2" etc. Then display.

Demonstrating Step 5

1. Begin with a folder containing at least some of the artists' names that the child learned in *Step 4.*

2. Proceed as in *Step 4* but now say the title as well as the artist's name on each Learning Card.

3. After considerable practice with each folder, encourage the child to match the Name Cards with the Learning Cards first and then use the Control Cards to check his work.

The Age of Innocence by Reynolds

The Lovers by Picasso

STEP **6** LEARNING ABOUT THE SCHOOLS OF ART

After a youngster can recognize the work of some of the major artists, he can begin to look at these artists as representatives of particular schools of art. A school of art is a group of artists whose paintings show a general similarity of style. They are often influenced by a particular region or country during a specific time period, such as the Seventeenth Century Dutch School. It is difficult for children, or even adults, to recognize the characteristics of various schools of art when they are looking at random selections of paintings. However, when they concentrate on examples of the work of six artists from the same school, they are often able to detect the similarities of style. It is exciting to observe children recognizing these similarities. I once heard a six year-old remark, "They all look a little blurry," as he formed a row of paintings by six Impressionist artists.

Kasimir Malevich
*Suprematist Composition:
Red Square and
Black Square*
Museum of Modern Art

STEP

6

Materials

• At least six gray pocket-folders. This number can increase to about 20 depending on how far you want to expand your project.

• A 5″x1″ poster board label for each artist in each folder.

• Six pairs of mounted identical paintings for each folder. Each pair is by a different artist, but all the paintings in each folder exhibit the characteristics of that particular school of art.

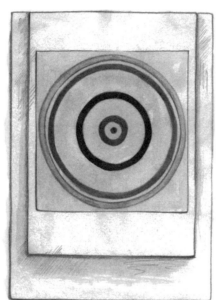

Kenneth Noland
Turnsole
Museum of Modern Art

Piet Mondrian
Broadway Boogie Woogie
Museum of Modern Art

Selecting the Schools of Art for Step 6

1. Before preparing the folders for *Step 6*, read the descriptions of the schools of art which start on page 52.

2. Begin with about six selected schools of art. The choice can be arbitrary depending on the art cards you have available, but it is most effective if all six schools are very different from each other. I have found the following to be one good initial selection:

> Seventeenth Century Dutch Paintings
> Impressionist Paintings
> Eighteenth Century British Portraits
> Geometric Abstract paintings
> Primitive Paintings
> Japanese Paintings

3. As alternates or additions to the first group of schools use any of the other schools of art described in the Appendix.

Note: Many of the names of the early Oriental and Primitive artists are not known. However, their paintings are so beautiful that they should be included in your *Step 6* folders, even though it is not possible to associate an artist's name with every painting.

Preparing the Sets

Each school of art has its own gray pocket-folder. Label each folder according to the school of art and paste a duplicate of one of the chosen paintings on the cover. For example,

Cubism. Place the Information Card in the left pocket and the Art Cards in the right pocket.

Demonstrating the Two Exercises for Step 6

1. The first exercise introduces children to the schools of art—the history of the movement, the distinguishing artistic style and the artists who are commonly associated with each style.

2. Begin with a folder containing some paintings which are familiar to the child.

3. Read or have the child read the Information card. Then arrange the Art Cards in a row and discuss the style of the paintings, the subject matter, etc.

4. Use the questions on the back of each card to focus on details of the paintings.

5. After the child is familiar with one school of art, proceed to the next one for further discussions and comparisons.

6. The second exercise, especially appropriate for younger children, is to match each painting with the name of the artist. To do this you may re-use your small gray pocket-folders with a corresponding Cover Card glued on the front. You will also need TWO copies of "Modern Schools of Art," (the volume of *Child-Size Masterpieces for Steps 6 & 7*) and you will need to cut the artists' name off the second set.

7. One volume will serve as the Control Cards and the other volume as the Learning Cards. Place the Control Cards in the left pocket and the Learning Cards and names in the right pocket.

8. Proceed to prepare and demonstrate this exercise following the instructions for *Step 4*.

Other Uses for These Step 6 Folders

It is worthwhile to make a considerable number of folders for *Step 6* because you will use them again for *Step 7* and *Step 8*. In addition, these schools of art folders are appropriate to use in a history, geography or cultural unit whenever children are studying a particular portion of history or a particular country of the world. For example, Early American paintings can be coordinated with a study of colonial or eighteenth century American history. Italian masters will be perfect illustrations for studying the Renaissance. And Oriental paintings are excellent visual aids for a study of China or Japan. You will find these school of art folders a delightful addition to any home or classroom environment.

STEP 7 GROUPING PAINTINGS FROM THE SAME SCHOOL OF ART

This is a sorting exercise to give children practice in distinguishing one school of art from another. The Control Cards from the folders of three schools of art are mixed together and the child sorts them by placing the cards from each school in a horizontal row.

Selecting Schools of Art
LEVEL 1

The easiest combinations are three schools which are very different from each other, e.g. British, Abstract and Japanese.

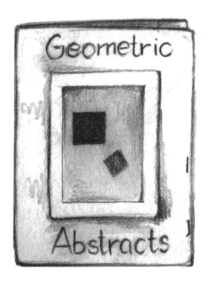

LEVEL 2

A more challenging combination is two schools which have some similarities and a contrasting one, e.g. American, Impressionism and Spanish.

LEVEL 3

The most challenging combination is three schools which are somewhat similar to each other, e.g. Surrealism, Cubism and Abstract.

Lawrence

Gainsborough

Mondrian

Noland

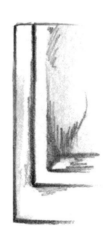

• An eight pocket black sorting folder (see page 44).

• At least three but preferably nine, *Step 6* folders, complete with mounted cards, for each level.

Increasing the Challenge by Rearranging

If you have folders for nine schools of art, you can probably use these for all three levels, simply by rearranging them. Many different combinations are possible. Following is just one example of how rearranging can increase the challenge at each Level:

Start with the easiest combinations for Level 1–

British Abstract Japanese
French Abstract Post-Impressionism
Dutch Cubist Impressionism

Rearrange these for a little more challenge for Level 2–

British Dutch Impressionism
French Surrealism Cubist
Abstract Post-Impressionism Japanese

Preparing the Exercise for Step 7

Make an eight pocket sorting folder. Stock this folder in the following way:

1. Select two or three school of art folders appropriate for the child's level.

2. Take one painting from each of the two (and later three or more) schools of art, mix them and put them in the first pocket of the sorting folder. Continue until seven pockets are filled.

3. Place the Information Cards in the eighth pocket.

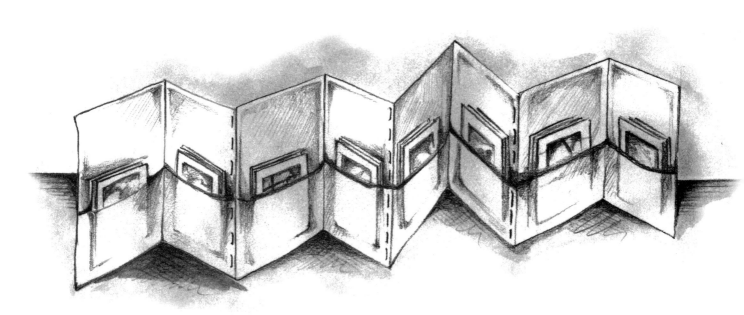

Rearrange again for the greatest challenge for Level 3–

| British
French
Dutch |

| Surrealism
Abstract
Cubist |

| Impressionism
Post-Impressionism
Japanese |

Demonstrating Step 7

The object of the exercise is to arrange the paintings from the black folder in horizontal rows, each headed by a gray folder identifying a school of art and beside it the Information Card for that school of art.

1. Place the two or three gray folders from which you have removed the Control Cards in a vertical row.

2. Remove the paintings from the first pocket of the black folder, and place each one beside the school of art folder to which it belongs.

3. Continue this procedure, using the cards from seven pockets, one pocket at a time.

Correcting Errors

One of the advantages of this exercise is that the person doing the exercise – teacher or child – can correct it herself if you have prepared the matching exercises for *Step 6*.

1. Remove the Learning Cards from the right-hand pocket of the first gray folder.
2. Lay each Learning Card on top of its identical Control Card in the first horizontal row.
3. If you have any Learning Card that does not match a Control Card in the first row, you know an error has been made and should be corrected.
4. Continue checking each row by the same procedure.
5. A simpler way of checking, if you have Information Cards, is to compare the names of the artists in each row with the artists' names on the reverse side of each of the Information Cards.
6. For further practice with names of the artists, match the Name Cards in each gray folder to the Learning Cards in each row, saying the artist's name aloud as you do so.
7. After completing the exercise, place the Control Cards from each horizontal row in the left-hand pocket of the gray folder to which they belong.
8. Place the Learning Cards and Name Cards from each row in the right-hand pocket of the appropriate folder. The black folder is now empty, ready to be used again.
8. Stock the black folder again and invite a child to do the exercise.

Expanding the Exercise

Add several more schools of art to the black folder, one school at a time. The child can then sort three, four, five and eventually six schools of art in this exercise.

A child will be able to do this advanced work only after a great deal of practice with the various schools of art. Never insist that a child memorize the names of the artists in a particular school of art. Let him come to know these artists gradually and naturally through frequent repetition of the exercises in *Step 6* and *Step 7*.

STEP 8 USING A TIME LINE

After a child has become familiar with a number of the important artists and schools of art, he can begin to locate them in history by placing art folders from *Step 6* or artcards along a Time Line. Essentially a Time Line is a long strip of paper or plastic about 10 to 15 inches wide on which a series of dates is printed at specific intervals. It is a very useful device for graphically illustrating art history or any other kind of history because it gives children a visual representation of consecutive events. To use a Time Line, a child must know how to read dates and understand their meaning.

Before making any of the Time Lines described below, read the detailed instructions on page 51. The length of any Time Line, as well as the span of its intervals, is determined by the subject and the period of history which it illustrates. For example, if you were making a Time Line of the Presidents of the United States, you would begin with 1789 and continue the dates at four-year intervals up to the present time. If you allowed four inches for every four-year interval, the Time Line would be about 18 feet long. A child working with this Time Line would stretch it out on the floor and put each president's picture and name beside the date when he took office.

Making Three Basic Time Lines

Time Lines of art history are not so evenly calibrated or as well defined. In my experience I have found that history of art can be best illustrated by three basic Time Lines, representing three consecutive periods of art history. Each of these Time Lines is calibrated differently to accommodate the volume of paintings from that portion of history.

1. Ancient and Medieval— This Time Line begins in 3000 B.C.E. and continues until 1300 C.E.—a period of 4300 years. Art that has survived from the early years of recorded history is dated by century rather than a specific year. Therefore five hundred year intervals are adequate for this early segment of history. Divide your Time Line into eleven equal segments. With a thick black marker print the title—*Ancient and Medieval Art*—in the first segment. Use a thick red marker to print the date 3000 B.C.E, 1500 B.C.E. 1000 B.C.E, 500 B.C.E. Print the remaining dates in the C.E period with a black marker: 1 C.E. 500 C.E, 1000 C.E. 1300 C.E.

2. Traditional Art— This Time Line begins with the Renaissance in 1300 and continues through 1850. Fifty-year intervals are used to accommodate the painting of this prolific period of 550 years. Divide your Time Line into thirteen equal segments. With a black marker print the title in the first segment and the following dates in the remaining segments: 1300, 1350, 1400, 1450, 1500, 1550, 1600, 1650, 1700, 1750, 1800, 1850.

3. Modern Art— This Time Line begins with the Impressionists in 1850 and continues to the present time. Since so many rapidly changing styles of Modern Art belong in this period, it is best displayed in ten-year intervals. With a black marker print the title in the first segment and the year 1850 in the second segment. Continue with every tenth year: 1860, 1870, 1880, etc., up to the present time.

OF ART

Some Special Time Lines

1. A Child's Own Time Line— A delightful way to introduce a child to history as the story of consecutive events is to help him make a Time Line of his own life with one segment for each year. This Time Line begins with the year of his birth beside which he can place the earliest photograph of himself—also pictures of his parents or other important people in his life during that year. Beside the second date, one year later, place his picture taken around the time of his first birthday. Continue these pictures to the present time including photographs of new brothers and sisters, new pet, new house, starting to school, vacations, etc. The child's mounted photographs may be kept in an orange folder with his picture on the cover and labeled with his name, e.g. "Michael's Time Line."

2. A Time Line of Pre-historic Painting— If the children with whom you work are interested in the Cave Paintings and you wish to dramatize how very old these paintings are, you can make a Pre-historic Time Line beginning with the year 20,000 B.C.E. and continuing until 3000 B.C.E. Use 1000-year intervals and print all dates in red. Place cards of the cave paintings beside the first few dates— 20,000 B.C.E., 19,000 B.C.E., 18,000 B.C.E., and then no more cards until the Egyptian tomb paintings in 3000 B.C.E. This Time Line graphically portrays the long intervening period from which we presently have very few surviving examples of painting.

3. A sequence of paintings by one particular artist— Five-year intervals should be used for an individual artist, beginning with the date of his or her earliest work. Picasso is the most obvious choice for an individual Time Line because he made many significant style changes during his long lifetime. In fact, a Time Line display is one of the most dramatic ways of looking at Picasso's work. Other artists whose paintings make interesting Time Lines are Matisse, Goya, Chagall and Monet.

Using Your Art Folders with the Basic Time Lines

For a child's initial Time Line exercise select one of the three basic Time Lines which will accommodate some of the folders of the schools of art which you prepared for *Step 6.* Show the child how to place each folder beside the Time Line near the date when that school was active. Later he can use all three Time Lines in sequence to accommodate all the folders which you have made. If you have a complete set beginning with the Egyptian tomb paintings and continuing through modern abstracts, the cover paintings on these folders will form a beautiful display of the consecutive major developments in art history.

Even if you have only a few of the school of art folders, it is worthwhile placing them on the Time Lines to give the child an idea of the sequential relationship of these schools to each other.

Later the child can use these same materials to make a much more elaborate display. He can remove the Control Cards from each folder and place them beside their appropriate dates in a horizontal row perpendicular to the Time Line. This impressive display will then feature about six examples from each school.

New Sequences for Your Basic Time Lines

Actually your *Step 6* materials are only the first of many delightful sequences that can be displayed on your Time Lines. Next I suggest you make orange folders containing artcards selected specifically to illustrate interesting developments in painting.

1. A sequence of paintings of a particular subject by artists from many countries over a lengthy period of time:

When one subject, such as "Mother and Child," is displayed on a Time Line, it is easy for a child to observe changes in the way this subject was painted through several centuries— differences in dress, differences in formality or informality, in backgrounds, in style, etc. These changes are noticeable only if every painting has the same subject matter. They are not nearly so evident if you use a random selection of subjects.

Any of the following are good subjects for a Time Line because each of them was painted by a great number of the important artists in history: Men, Women, Children, Landscapes, Still Lifes, Mothers and Children, and Musicians.

The subject of Musicians—not portraits of composers but paintings of persons playing musical instruments—is particularly interesting. Because a Time Line of Musicians shows the very old instruments such as lutes and harpsichords, it is fun to coordinate this Time Line with listening to some of the music written for these instruments during a particular time in history.

2. A sequence of paintings from a particular country, such as "Spanish Painting from El Greco to Dali" or "American Painting from Colonial Times to the Present."

This sequence can be used for many different countries, especially Italy, France, Germany, England, China and Japan. It is particularly effective for illustrating the many changes in the style of American art in a relatively short period of history. See pages 65-68. Both of the sequences described above can be used with your three basic Time Lines.

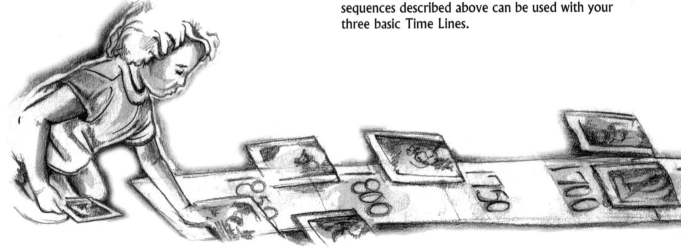

Preparing Folders for New Sequences

When preparing art cards for your orange pocket-folders, print the name of the artist and the date of the painting on the front of each mounting card. This date is usually found on the reverse side of the postcard. If the date of the painting is not included with the information there, use the dates of the artist's life and put them in parentheses. When placing the card beside the Time Line, assume that the date of the painting would be some time after the mid-point of the artist's life.

Prepare your double orange folder according to the directions on page 50. Not all sequences will have exactly 24 paintings. To determine the number of folders to be stapled together for one sequence allow one folder for each 12 artcards. Mix up the sequential order of the dates before storing the mounted cards in the pockets. Place a directly related artcard on the cover and label each folder according to its subject. For example, *Time Line of Men* or *Time Line of American Art.*

Demonstrating the Time Line

It is fun to do a Time Line with two, three or four youngsters:

1. Let the children help you to unroll or unfold the Time Line carefully.

2. Explain that the Time line will enable them to see the consecutive order of paintings and/or schools of art from a long time ago up to more recent times.

3. Have the children read some of the dates and explain the number of years represented by the space between each date.

4. Remove a child-size masterpiece from an orange folder. Read its date aloud and then place it beside the Time Line within the appropriate time span.

5. Do the same with several more cards and then give each child a card to place beside the Time Line.

6. Divide the remaining cards among the children and let them finish the Time Line, making sure they read each date aloud.

7. Whenever several cards belong in the same time span, place them in a horizontal row, perpendicular to the Time Line. If your collection of art cards is a balanced representation of each important school of art, these rows will graphically illustrate periods of high productivity. Conversely, there will be no cards or only a few cards for years of low productivity or periods from which very few examples have survived.

8. If possible, let the finished Time Line remain in place for several hours, or even several days, so the children can absorb the details and talk about them.

9. When you are ready to put the Time Line away, show the children how to mix up the order of the cards and replace them in pockets of the orange folder. Then let the youngsters help you to roll or fold the Time Line carefully for storage.

HOW TO MOUNT YOUR ART POSTCARDS

1. Use a large paper cutter to cut sixteen mounting cards from a standard 22" X 28" sheet of medium weight white posterboard.

2. Center each art postcard left to right on each mounting card.

3. Put the top edge of each art postcard at the top edge of each mounting card leaving a one inch margin at the bottom for identification.

4. Access to information on the reverse side of the art postcard can be maintained if the postcard is hinged to the mounting card. Use a good quality wide tape to make a 3" hinge. Attach this hinge to the reverse side of the art postcard and the front of the mounting card as shown.

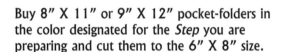

HOW TO MAKE SMALL POCKET FOLDERS

Buy 8" X 11" or 9" X 12" pocket-folders in the color designated for the *Step* you are preparing and cut them to the 6" X 8" size.

1. With the folder closed, measure to a point 8" above the bottom edge and 6" from the left or folded edge.

2. From this point draw a 6" horizontal line to the folded edge and an 8" vertical line to the bottom edge.

3. Cut the closed folder on these lines.

4. Use staples to close the outside edge of each pocket where it was cut off.

5. When making a double folder for *Step 3* or *Step 8* attach the back cover of one folder to the front cover of a second folder with paste and reinforce this with staples.

6. Paste a beautiful art postcard, called a Cover Card on the front of each folder.

Note: Small 6" X 8" vinyl folders are available in colors appropriate for *Steps 1-8* from Parent Child Press.

50

HOW TO MAKE AND USE TIME LINES

Use a roll of 12″ white paper or computer paper folded accordion-style on creases. Print one date on each 12″ section. A folded Time Line has the advantage of lying flat on the floor and folding easily for storage. However, unless it is handled carefully, it may tear on the folds.

Children are most comfortable using a Time Line on the floor because it is very easy for them to place any number of art postcards beside it. However, a Time Line project on the floor takes a great deal of space, and it is often not practical to leave it on display for more than a few hours or a few days.

A Time Line on the wall can usually remain in place for longer periods. It should be mounted horizontally at a height which is convenient for the children who will use it. If you hang the Time Line directly above a chalk tray or above a long shelf, the children can stand the Child-Size Masterpieces on the chalk tray or shelf and lean them against their appropriate dates on the Time line. If you have no chalk tray or long shelf available, then mount the Time Line on the wall at floor level and the children can lay the cards on the floor in front of it.

A Time Line which can be mounted horizontally on the wall or used on the floor.

A SAMPLE OF MANUSCRIPT LETTERING

The manuscript lettering illustrated below is a good clear style to use when you are printing on mounting cards or folders.

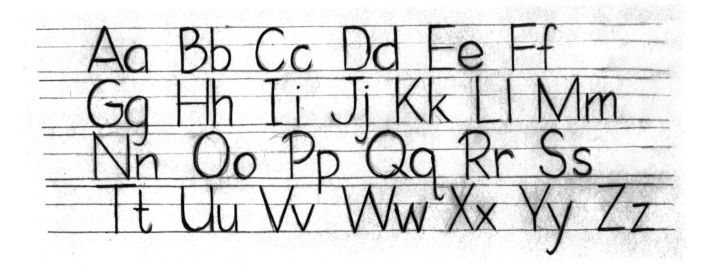

THE SCHOOLS OF ART IN HISTORY

Altar Piece
King Balthasar
Barcelona
12th Century

The following summaries of some of the important schools in art history are for your own quick reference when you are preparing the art card activities, presenting them to children and answering their questions.

Because this entire project is designed for children, I have simplified these descriptions as much as possible. In no way are they intended to be complete or definitive. The history of art is long and complicated. A detailed knowledge is helpful but certainly not essential for working with *Child-Size Masterpieces*.

A school of art is a group of artists whose paintings show a general similarity of style because they shared a particular influence during a specific time period. Because classifying the work of painters is not an exact science many art reference books differ in the way they delineate the schools of art and the selection of artists that are included. The style of some painters is so individual that they cannot be classified in any of the commonly recognized schools, and the style of others, particularly modern artists, is so varied that they are included in two or three different schools.

It is important to understand that the making of art is a continuous process with artists borrowing techniques or taking inspiration from what has gone before them. Some artists build on the work of those who immediately preceded them while others reach back through the centuries for their models. Thus many modern painters owe more to primitive art than to the formalities of later European painting.

For convenience, I have divided the history of art into three segments which will correspond to the three basic Time Lines mentioned in earlier sections of this text. These divisions are Ancient and Medieval Art from 3000 B.C.E. to 1300 C.E. Traditional Art from 1300 to 1850 and Modern Art from 1850 to present. Preceding these three divisions of recorded history are the Cave Paintings.

PREHISTORIC ART

The Cave Paintings

The earliest known paintings are the Cave Paintings which date back to about 20,000 B.C.E. They were discovered during the past one hundred years on the walls of caves in France and Spain. The Cave Paintings have a simple flat appearance and each one usually features a single animal. Sometimes this animal is one that no longer exists or else lives only in regions much further north. The artists used paints made from clay and stones, limiting the colors to the earth tones.

These pre-historic paintings have survived because they were preserved in the darkness and special atmospheric conditions which exist deep within caves or tombs. Very few examples of painting have been discovered from the long period of approximately 14,000 years which followed the Cave Paintings.

Paleolithic painting
Female Bison
Cave of Altamira

ANCIENT AND MEDIEVAL ART

Although much more detailed and elaborate than the Cave Paintings, the paintings from 3000 B.C.E. to 1300 C.E. were limited to the same two-dimensional appearance because the technique of perspective and the use of shadows had not yet been adequately developed.

Egyptian Paintings

Recorded history began in Egypt about 3000 B.C.E. Much of it was revealed to us through the discovery of elaborate tombs which had been prepared for kings and noblemen. The walls of the rooms inside the tombs were covered with paintings of everyday life—hunting, fishing, harvesting, eating, playing music, dancing, making jewelry, cutting hair, attending a party and many other activities. Most of the faces are shown in profile with the shoulders facing front, indicating that these artists had difficulty drawing a full face or a side view of the shoulder. Most of the women in the paintings are wearing black wigs and their skin is painted a much lighter color than that of the men. Indeed most of the women look alike and most of the men look alike, since the artists made no attempt to portray any individual characteristics.

Egyptian tomb painting
Guests and Musicians
18th Dynasty

Paintings from Crete

The Palace of Minos was discovered in recent years on the island of Crete. Paintings on its walls portray animals, flowers, birds and imaginary scenes, as well as human figures. Here the men are also painted with skin darker than the women, but both men and women are freer and more graceful than in the Egyptian paintings. This art dates from 2000 B.C.E to 1200 C.E Other wall paintings depicting scenes of hunts and battles have been discovered in the Palace of Mycenae and the Palace of Tiryns.

Greek, Etruscan and Roman Painting

From the seventh to the third century B.C.E. the Greeks produced their finest thinkers and artists. Because many famous examples of sculpture and architecture from this period still survive, we tend to speak of the masterpieces of Greek art as temples and statues. Painting, however, was equally important at the time. Unfortunately, all the paintings which decorated the walls of the temples have been destroyed. The only remaining examples of Greek painting from this famous period are the beautiful "vase paintings" with which they decorated their pottery.

Some experts believe that the lost paintings of the Greeks may have resembled the Etruscan tomb paintings which date from the fifth century B.C.E. The Etruscans, who lived in what is now central Italy, were great admirers of the Greeks. The figures in their paintings are well proportioned and have an almost three dimensional appearance.

Both the Greeks and the Etruscans influenced the art of the Romans who conquered them. Many of the Roman wall paintings from the first century B.C.E. and the first century C.E survive because of a catastrophe—they were buried, and thus preserved, by the eruption of Vesuvius in 79 C.E. These paintings, located in Pompeii, Herculaneum and Stabiae, include landscapes, portraits, still lifes and garden scenes. Some have an airy quality that is almost impressionistic.

The tomb paintings in the city of Rome which date from the early centuries C.E are known as the Catacomb Paintings and are the first paintings to exhibit Christian themes.

Painting in the Middle Ages

During the Middle Ages the monasteries and the churches kept the arts alive in Europe when most of that continent was engulfed in wars, plagues and poverty. From the 5th century C.E. to about the 15th century C.E. Western Art was almost entirely influenced by early Christianity, which used paintings as a means of teaching the Gospels. These paintings were often done on wet plaster in churches or on wooden altar pieces. When done on wet plaster they were called *frescoes.* Illustrations of gospel stories were also included in *illuminated manuscripts* painted by monks. The most famous of the illuminated manuscripts is the *Book of Kells* from the 8th century which contains some of the most intricate designs ever made and is decorated with gold leaf. The figures, however, like those in the Egyptian paintings have no body contours or depth.

Book of Kells
The Virgin and Child
Late 8th Century

TRADITIONAL EUROPEAN ART

What is frequently referred to as "Traditional Art" began with the use of perspective in the 14th century and extended to the beginning of Modern Art in 1850. The early centuries of Traditional Art continued to serve the work of Christianity so that religious themes predominated.

Italian Renaissance

Near the end of the 14th century a great change came about in Europe, a change which has been called *Renaissance*, meaning re-birth. Inspired by growth in trade, travel, nationalism and learning, this period, which is known for its rich development in culture and art, began in Florence, Italy. Here master artists taught young apprentices to mix paint for frescoes and tempera—a sort of water color thickened with egg yolks—which was used to paint altar pieces on wooden boards. Oil paint was not in use during the early Renaissance.

The earliest artist to make human figures life-like was Giotto, who actually preceded the Renaissance by one hundred years. His figures were not perfect but they were rounded rather than flat, and they had human expressions on their faces. Giotto's backgrounds, however, had no real depth.

For the next two centuries one great artist followed another. These great Italian Renaissance painters studied anatomy so thoroughly that they were able to portray the human body perfectly in any position. They also mastered the techniques of perspective enabling them to depict objects at any distance from the eye of the viewer. Three of the greatest artists of the Italian Renaissance were Leonardo da Vinci, who was renowned for his accurate scientific drawings as well as his paintings; Raphael Sanzio, who was known for the beauty of his composition and figures; and Michelangelo, who executed the monumental paintings on the ceiling of the Sistine Chapel in Rome.

Michelangelo
Head of Etruscan Sibyl
Sistine Chapel, Rome

Italian Renaissance Painters
Early Renaissance—14th-15th centuries
Giotto di Bondone 1266-1337
Fra Angelico 1387-1455
Fra Filippo Lippi 1406-1469
Pierro della Francesco 1416-1492
Sandro Botticelli 1444-1510 .

High Renaissance—16th century
Leonardo da Vinci 1452-1519
Michelangelo Buonarroti 1475-1564
Titain (Tiziano Vecellio) 1477-1576
Antonio Allegri Correggio 1495-1534
Raphael Sanzio 1483-1520
Jacopo Tintoretto 1518-1594

Northern Renaissance Painting

At the time of the Italian Renaissance, another group of outstanding painters were working in Flanders (now Belgium) and the area now known as Germany. Their work is often referred to as Northern Renaissance painting.

The earliest of the great Flemish painters was Jan van Eyck, whose painting *The Annunciation* is a marvel of perspective. He was the first to mix powdered color with an oil base rather than an egg base, thus inventing the slow-drying oil paint used by all great masters who followed him. Unlike the formerly used tempera which had dried so quickly, the oil paint could be blended on the canvas. While the Renaissance painters of Italy made a special study of the anatomy of the body and the portrayal of movement, the painters of the north specialized in studying the surface of everything they painted—its texture, color and the effect of light on it—and they carefully put every tiny detail on their canvases. Rubens is particularly noted for his beautiful skin textures and the Bruegels for their detailed scenes with many people.

The great German painter, Dürer, who was also a scientist and an engraver, is renowned for exact details such as fur of animals and perfectly drawn muscles. The two Holbeins were famous for the extraordinary beauty of their portraits.

German Painters
Albrecht Dürer 1471-1528
Hans Holbein, the Younger 1497-1543
Lukas Cranch, the Elder 1472-1553
Ambrosius Holbein 1494-1520
Albrecht Altdorfer 1480-1538

Flemish Painters
Peter Paul Rubens 1577-1640
Jacob Jordaens 1593-1678
Rogier van der Weyden 1400-1464
Hans Memling 1435-1494
Hieronymus Bosch 1450-1516
Pieter Bruegel the Elder 1525-1569
Jan Bruegel 1568-1625
Jan van Eyck 1385-1441
Anthony van Dyck 1599-1641
Jan Gossaert 1478-1533

Rogier Van der Weyden
Portait of a Lady
National Gallery of Art,
Washington DC

Spanish Painting, 16th to 18th Century

Spain's first great painter, known as El Greco, was actually a Greek who lived in Spain during the 16th century. El Greco's paintings can be recognized by their distortion. He deliberately elongated and twisted his human figures to make them more dramatic. In the next generation the greatest painter was Velasquez who served as the artist for the king's court and was known for the perfect likenesses of his portraits. He was followed by Murillo, whose work included religious scenes on very large canvases and street scenes showing urchins eating and playing games. One hundred years after Velasquez, the Spanish court had another great artist—Goya—whose portraits did not flatter his subjects but mocked them in caricature. He also painted scenes of daily life and was noted for his etchings of beasts and monsters.

Seventeenth Century Dutch Painting

Instead of religious themes, the 17th century Dutch painters portrayed the new middle-class society in portraiture and scenes from daily life. DeHooch painted warm family scenes (which often included a geometric pattern of floor tiles) and Vermeer featured portraits of women quietly working. The roisterous life of the tavern was portrayed by Hals and Metsu. Both Rembrandt and Ruisdael created spectacular lighting in their landscapes. Rembrandt, of course, surpassed all the other artists with his profound portraiture. While other 17th century artists painted people's outward appearance, Rembrandt was concerned with the depth of the human soul, revealing both its grandeur and its misery in dramatic encounters of light and dark. It is remarkable that so many great artists lived and worked in the tiny country of Holland during this short period of time.

Velasquez
Don Baltasar Carlos
The Wallace Collection
London

Spanish Painters

El Greco 1541-1614	Diego Velásquez 1599-1660
Jusepe da Ribera 1590-1652	Bartolomé Murillo 1617-1682
Francisco Zurbarán 1598-1664	Francisco de Goya 1746-1828

Dutch Painters

Frans Hals 1580-1666	Jacob van Ruisdael 1628-1682
Rembrandt van Rijn 1606-1669	Gabriel Metsu 1629-1667
Gerard Ter Borch 1617-1681	Pieter de Hooch 1629-1688
Aelbert Cuyp 1620-1691	Johannes Vermeer 1632-1675
Jan Steen 1626-1679	Judith Leyster 1610-1660
	Meindert Hobbema 1638-1709

Johannes Vermeer
The Kitchen-maid
Rijksmuseum, Amsterdam

18th Century French Painting

French painters in the 18th century often depicted the carefree life of courtiers—beautiful maidens and handsome youths amusing themselves. This art can be characterized as idyllic, portraying life romantically rather than realistically. Because the French preferred delicate, soft lines and pastel colors, these 18th century paintings have sometimes been criticized as being more *pretty* than beautiful. The greatest painter of palace life was Watteau, who often portrayed traveling companies of actors. In the next generation Boucher was noted for his portraits of ladies of the court and Fragonard for his graceful figures in landscapes with soaring trees and puffy white clouds. Chardin, on the other hand, painted the simple home life of the people.

Fragonard *The Swing*
The Wallace Collection, London

French Painters

Antoine Watteau 1684-1721
Jean Baptiste Chardin 1699-1779
François Boucher 1703-1770
Jean Baptiste Perroneau 1715-1783
Jean Baptiste Greuze 1725-1805
François Drouais 1727-1775
Jean-Honoré Fragonard 1732-1806

British Painters

William Hogarth 1697-1764
Joshua Reynolds 1723-1792
Thomas Gainsborough 1727-1788
George Romney 1734-1802
Henry Raeburn 1756-1823
Thomas Lawrence 1769-1830

18th Century British Painting

Until the 18th century, the British felt that all good art must come from abroad. Hogarth was the first English artist to prove that an Englishman could paint as well as a foreigner. Hogarth's subjects were the common people and his portrayal of them in their everyday work was a social comment on his times.

The work of the portrait artists who followed Hogarth had a much different look. These artists—Reynolds, Gainsborough, Romney and Lawrence—painted the wealthy people who commissioned portraits for their homes. In these portraits the subjects were usually dressed lavishly but their costumes were not always indicative of the style of that time. Many of their portraits of children have become favorites around the world.

Joshua Reynolds
The Age of Innocence
Tate Gallery, London

Nineteenth Century Romanticism, Realism and Neoclassicism

In the first half of the nineteenth century a new spirit of non-conformity and artistic freedom influenced the work of European painters. Known as Romanticism, this movement covered a wide range of subjects—landscapes, seascapes, portraits, drama, mythological scenes and mystical works. Each of the Romantic painters had a very individual style. Constable's landscapes and Turner's seascapes subdue concrete details with the drama of wind, sunlight and clouds. Blake, who was obsessed with Milton, Dante and the Bible, created mystical drawings which were highly symbolic. The movement flourished in both England and France, but perhaps the greatest of all Romantic painters was Francisco de Goya of Spain.

With the new scientific developments of the second half of the nineteenth century, Romanticism declined in popularity. Three Frenchmen—Courbet, Daumier and Millet—were the greatest of the new Realists who portrayed everyday life with frankness and authenticity.

Neoclassicism was a less important movement that abandoned elaborate detail in favor of the clean style of ancient Roman and Greek sculpture.

Francisco de Goya
Grape-gathering

Romantic Painters

Francisco de Goya 1746-1828
William Blake 1757-1827
J.M.W. Turner 1775-1851
John Constable 1776-1837
Camille Corot 1796-1875
Eugene Delacroix 1798-1863
Theodore Géricault 1791-1824
Theodore Rousseau 1821-1867

Realist Painters

Gustave Courbet 1819-1877
François Millet 1814-1875
Honoré Daumier 1808-1879

Neoclassicist Painters

Jacques Louis David 1748-1825
Antoine Gros 1771-1835
Jean-Auguste Ingres 1780-1867

MODERN ART

In the mid 19th century a new era of art began which led step by step from the realistic representations of traditional art through a variety of contemporary schools and arrived ultimately at completely abstract art in which no real persons or objects can be identified.

Auguste Renoir *A Girl With A Watering Can*
National Gallery of Art, Washington DC

Impressionism

Impressionism is the great turning point from traditional painting to modern art. It began in France about 1860 and flourished there for about twenty years. The Impressionist painters turned away from the strict representation of reality and produced instead a somewhat blurry image or an "impression" of a subject. To do this they abandoned the careful preparation which had been customary in the indoor studios and moved their canvases outdoors where they could spontaneously paint their perceptions of nature. For example, when painting a garden they no longer neatly outlined every flower, leaf and stem. Instead they painted what they actually saw— bright splashes of color. They were also fascinated with the ever-changing outdoor light and sometimes made several paintings of the same scene, each at a different time of day. By subduing the details of their subject matter, the Impressionists paved the way for the more abstract art of the 20th century.

French Impressionist Painters

Camille Pissarro 1830-1903
Edgar Degas 1834-1917
Claude Monet 1840-1926
Berthe Morisot 1841-1895
Edouard Manet 1832-1883
Alfred Sisley 1839-1899
Pierre Auguste Renoir 1841-1919

Post-Impressionism

Post-Impressionism is not one particular style but a name for several different styles, all of which developed as reactions against Impressionism. The artists were French or worked in France from about 1880 to about 1910. Because they felt that Impressionism was too limiting, the Post-Impressionists innovated in several different ways. Georges Seurat and Paul Signac used *pointillism,*

Van Gogh
The Starry Night
Museum of Modern Art
New York

that is painting with separate dots of pure color so that the mixing of colors takes place in the eye of the viewer. Toulouse-Lautrec's cabaret scenes were tinged with caricature. Deep emotion characterized the paintings of both Van Gogh, who used thick, surging, twisting strokes, and Gauguin, who used broad, simple flat tones. One of the most important Post-Impressionists, Cézanne, stressed the geometric structures that make up many scenes in nature and thereby began to formalize the casual character of Impressionism. His emphasis on these geometric patterns led the way to Cubism.

Paul Gauguin
Crouching Tahitian Girl
Art Institute of Chicago

Post Impressionist Painters

Paul Cézanne 1839-1906	Gustave Moreau 1826-1898	Paul Gauguin 1848-1903
Georges Seurat 1859-1891	Maurice Utrillo 1883-1955	Pierre Bonnard 1867-1947
Paul Signac 1863-1935	Vincent Van Gogh 1853-1890	Odilon Redon 1840-1916
Edouard Vuillard 1868-1940	Henri de Toulouse-Lautrec 1864-1901	

Fauvism

Fauvism was the first defiant movement in the 20th century. The name, given to the group by a Paris art critic, is derived from the French words *Les Fauves* meaning *the wild beasts*. The strongest characteristic of the Fauvists was their bold—and often garish—use of color. Precise drawing gave way to simplification and to color-conveyed emotion which appeared *wild* to the critics.

Fauvism was short-lived, but it served as a stepping-off point for many famous artists who then went to Cubism or developed their own individual styles. Georges Rouault painted religious subjects in colors separated by heavy black lines resembling the lead of stained glass windows; Raoul Dufy's toned-down colors seemed to express delight in a deft, highly personal style. The greatest of the Fauves, Henri Mattisse, achieved great harmony and brilliance of color in a concise and economical style that often expressed joy in life.

Fauvists Painters

Henri Matisse 1869-1954
André Derain 1880-1954
Raoul Dufy 1877-1953
Maurice de Vlaminck 1876-1958
Georges Rouault 1871-1958
Albert Marquet 1875-1947

Henri Matisse
Dance (First Version)
The Museum of Modern Art, New York

Pablo Picasso
The Pond in Horta de Ebro
Coleccion Particular, Paris

Cubism

The Cubist movement led by Picasso and Braque began in France in 1907 and lasted until about 1920. It still influences contemporary art. Throughout history all painters have had to deal with the problem of portraying a three-dimensional world on a flat two-dimensional surface. The Cubist's solution to this problem was looking at a single image from many aspects and putting all the aspects on one canvas in a geometric arrangement of blocks, lines and angles. For example, they often portrayed a full face and its profile at the same time, sometimes overlapping the face with other parts of the body so that the finished product suggested motion. In addition to the human figure, the Cubists also used objects as their points of departure—violins, guitars, bowls of fruit, etc. Because of their preoccupation with form, the early Cubists played down color, often using neutral shades of brown, gray or tan. Their emphasis on form, rather than subject, gave modern art its great push toward abstraction.

Pablo Picasso
The Pond in Horta de Ebro
Coleccion Particular, Paris

Cubists Painters

Pablo Picasso 1881-1973
Juan Gris 1887-1927
Fernand Leger 1881-1955
Francis Picabia 1878-1953
George Braque 1882-1963
Marcel Duchamp 1887-1968
Robert Delaunay 1885-1941

Abstract Art

Purely abstract painting was initiated by Wassily Kandinsky in Munich in 1910. The abstract artists decided to give up the long tradition of painting real things, scenes or people. Instead they used colors, lines, patterns and other effects which produced no resemblance at all to natural objects or persons. This sharp break with the past required viewers to learn to look at paintings as combinations of form and color or as graphic representations of emotions or moods. Although it started in Europe, some of the most significant abstract painting has been done in the United States in what is called the New York School. See American Painting, page 67. There are two main currents of abstract art:

Geometric Abstract Art is characterized by lines, either straight or curved, logical patterns and various geometric shapes. Some European geometric abstract artists are:

Piet Mondrian 1872-1944
Kasimir Malevich 1878-1935
Antoine Pevsner 1886-1962

Piet Mondrian
Composition, 1921

Non-geometric Abstract Art has no definable patterns. It is spontaneous and emotional compared to the carefully planned design of geometric abstracts. Its irregular appearance, sometimes resembling the drawings of children, often seems to convey either suppressed or impetuous feelings. Some European abstract painters are:

Wassily Kandinsky 1866-1944
Paul Klee 1879-1940
Kurt Schwitters 1887-1948
Hans Arp 1888-1966
Max Ernst 1891-1976
Joan Miró 1893-1983
Ben Nicholson 1894-1982
André Masson 1896-1987
Jean Dubuffet 1901-1985
Karel Appel 1921-2006

Joan Miró, *Woman and Little Girl in Front of the Sun,*
Hirshhorn Museum
Washington DC

Surrealism

Surrealism began in Paris in 1924 and continued through the 1930's. Greatly influenced by Sigmund Freud, the Surrealists explored their subconscious minds and based their paintings on dreams, hallucinations, fantasies and symbolism. They often used real images in distorted or unreal settings in their efforts to put on canvas the secret life of the mind. Closely related to the Surrealists and included with them in this manual are the Fantasy Artists—particularly Marc Chagall who greatly enriched painting with his colorful, topsy-turvy, fairy-tale-like canvases.

Surrealist Painters

Salvador Dali 1904-1989
Joan Miró 1893-1983
René Magritte 1898-1967
Yves Tanguey 1900-1955
Max Ernst 1891-1976
Marc Chagall 1887-1985
Georgio De Chirico
    1888-1978
Paul Klee 1879-1940
André Masson 1896-1987

Marc Chagall
Green Viloinist
The Solomon R. Guggenheim Museum
New York

Salvador Dali
Persistence of Memory

Expressionism

Influenced by the horror of World War 1, the Expressionist painters portrayed anguish and torment of the spirit. Their art was a reaction against what they felt was the unreal serenity of Impressionism. Using powerful distortions and harsh, violent colors, they attempted to portray the troubled inner soul rather than the physical world they saw with their eyes. Expressionism had its roots in the work of El Greco and Van Gogh and it developed powerfully in the paintings of the Norwegian, Edvard Munch. Expressionism flourished as a movement in Germany in the early part of the twentieth century.

Primitive or Naïve Painters

Primitive painters are usually self-taught artists who use a simple *naïve* style for painting portraits, landscapes, many-peopled scenes and historical events. The word *naïve* means showing natural simplicity or being without experience and information. Because they lacked formal training and familiarity with the works of recognized artists, these painters often omitted the shadows and gradations that usually give dimension to objects on a canvas. Also, they did not use perspective to relate the different items in a scene to each other. Nevertheless their paintings are direct and sincere and many of them show a masterful use of color.

Individual Primitive artists are found throughout art history. They were not a group working at a particular time in a particular place. Some of the artists' names are not known, even though their works hang in museums. The most famous Primitive artist is Henri Rousseau, whose work was discovered by Picasso.

Primitive Painters

Henri Rousseau 1844-1910
Edward Hicks 1780-1849
John Kane 1860-1934
Linton Park 1826-1906
Horace Pippin 1888-1946
Grandma Moses 1860-1961
John Bradley (active) 1832-1847
Clementine Hunter 1887-1988

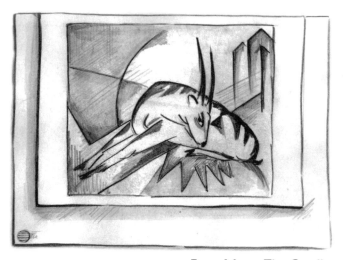

Franz Marc, *The Gazelle*
Rhode Island School
of Design Museum

Expressionist Painters

James Ensor 1860-1949
Edvard Munch 1863-1944
Alexei Jawlensky 1864-1941
Emil Nolde 1867-1956
Paul Klee 1879-1940
Ernst Ludwig Kirchner 1880-1938
Franz Marc 1880-1916
Max Pechstein 1881-1955
Karl Schmidt-Rottluff 1884-1976
Oskar Kokoschka 1886-1983
August Macke 1887-1914

John Bradley, *Little Girl*
National Gallery of Art
Washington DC

AMERICAN PAINTING

The history of American Painting is a panorama of many different styles, some of which reflect those used in Europe. Unlike the Europeans, however, American painters had no demand for the palace scenes and religious subjects favored in Europe. They worked under the patronage of a middle-class society, and they painted their own people in familiar scenes of everyday life.

Pre-Colonial Years

The earliest painting in the land that is now the United States was done by the Native Americans, often as decorations on pottery. These artists used colorful earth tones to make intricate designs which sometimes had a zig-zag pattern. Their paintings also featured birds, animals, heads, headdresses, etc. Completely free of the tradition of Christianity, these **Native American** artists used their own unique symbols to reflect the Great Spirit which they believed inhabited all of nature and influenced their personal lives.

17th and 18th Centuries

Portraits done by the early European settlers in the seventeenth century were **Primitive** in style and those of the early eighteenth century were copies of styles used in England. However, in the mid-eighteenth century four famous native-born artists developed their own styles of painting portraits and scenes rather than imitating those of Europe:

Benjamin West 1738-1820
John Singleton Copley 1738-1815
Charles Willson Peale 1741-1827
Gilbert Stuart 1755-1828

Gilbert Stuart
George Washington
Sterling and Francine Clark Art Institute
Williamstown, MA

19th Century

Much of the painting in nineteenth century America featured the **Romantic** style because people who wanted to escape from their everyday lives enjoyed scenes of faraway places. Artists of the **Hudson River School** portrayed realistic landscapes in an idyllic manner:

Washington Allston 1779-1843
Samuel F.B. Morse 1791-1872
Asher Durand 1796-1886
Thomas Cole 1801-1848
George Inness 1825-1894
Frederic Church 1826-1900

But not all nineteenth century people enjoyed the romantic escape into a perfect dream world. Many were fascinated with the everyday world around them portrayed by the **Realists** (also called **Genre Painters**). These included:

> William Sidney Mount 1807-1868
> George Caleb Bingham 1811-1879
> Winslow Homer 1836-1910
> Thomas Eakins 1844-1916

Meanwhile some artist adventurers travelled west to paint the wilderness, the wildlife, the unspoiled Rocky Mountains, cowboys and Native Americans. Some of the **Western Painters** and their subjects are:

> John Audubon 1786-1851 birds
> George Catlin 1796-1872 Native Americans
> Albert Bierstadt 1830-1902 mountain scenes
> Frederic Remington 1861-1909 cowboys and horses
> Charles M. Russell 1864-1926 cowboys and horses

Winslow Homer
The Boat Builders
Indianapolis Museum of Art

Naïve **painting** continued in the nineteenth century with the work of several artists of whom the most famous was Edward Hicks, 1780-1849.

In the late nineteenth century several American painters used the **Impressionist** style popular in Paris:

> James McNeill Whistler 1834-1903
> Mary Cassatt 1845-1926
> William Merritt Chase 1849-1916
> John Singer Sargent 1856-1925
> Childe Hassam 1859-1933
> Henry O. Tanner 1859-1937

Frederic Remington
The Cowboy
Amon Carter museum, Fort Worth

Mary Cassatt
The Bath
The Art Institute of Chicago

20th Century

Twentieth century American art offers a rich variety of styles. In the early years a group called **The Eight** painted very commonplace subjects that were often rejected from the traditional exhibitions. Because of their depiction of the seamy side of life, they earned the nickname of **The Ash Can School.** However, this term belies the beauty of many of their paintings. The most well-known of *The Eight* were:

    Maurice Prendergast 1859-1924
    Robert Henri 1865-1929
    George Luks 1867-1933
    William Glackens 1870-1938
    John Sloan 1871-1951
    George Bellows 1882-1925 (associated with
        The Eight but not a member)

Because the United States is such a large country, **Regionalism** has always been a strong force and remains so today. Some Regionalist painters who used homegrown subject matter were:

    Thomas Hart Benton 1889-1975
    Grant Wood 1892-1941
    John Steuart Curry 1897-1946

Some twentieth century American **Realists** are:

    Edward Hopper 1882-1967
    Rockwell Kent 1882-1971
    Charles Burchfield 1893-1967
    Norman Rockwell 1894-1978
    Andrew Wyeth 1917-
    Alice Neel 1900-1984

With the coming of World War II many artists fled Europe and New York became a major center for contemporary art. The names **Abstract Expressionists** and **New York School** are used to describe many modern American artists, even though they have little in common with each other. Some who use compulsive movement are:

    Stuart Davis 1894-1964
    Wilem de Kooning 1904-1997
    Hans Hofmann 1880-1966
    Robert Rauschenberg 1925-
    Jackson Pollock 1912-1956
    Larry Rivers 1923-2002
    Mark Tobey 1890-1976
    Roy Lichtenstein 1923-1997

Grant Wood
American Gothic
The Art Institute of Chicago

Robert Rauschenberg
Summer Rental, Number 2
Whitney Museum, New York

Others focus on all-prevailing color:
      Barnett Newman 1905-1970
      Mark Rothko 1903-1969
      Morris Louis 1912-1962
      Sam Francis 1923-1994
      Helen Frankenthaler 1928-
And still others offer geometric designs:
      Josef Albers 1888-1976
      Ellsworth Kelly 1923-
      Frank Stella 1936-
      Kenneth Noland 1924-

Pop Art is another twentieth century American style which portrays everyday objects, such as soup cans, in a very realistic manner. The most well-known Pop Artist is Andy Warhol 1928-1987.

The mid-twentieth century American artists have not yet stood the test of time. Some of them will hold a significant place in the art history to be written in the future; others will be forgotten or recorded as only minor artists. The 1960's and 1970's in American Art have been crowded with many different types of painting competing for attention, such as Pop Art, Op Art, Minimalism, Conceptualism and Photo-realism. It remains for history to decide if any of these movements will ever become an actual school of art.

Mexican Art

Of all the modern nations in North and South America, Mexico has the oldest and richest artistic heritage. Beautiful pottery, sculpture, architecture, and wall paintings survive from a variety of highly developed native cultures which flourished in Mexico during specific periods from ancient times until the Spanish conquest in the sixteenth century. Then Western-style art with its predominantly Christian themes was widely used to decorate churches and other public buildings. A wave of nationalism began with the Revolution of 1910 and three great muralists—Rivera, Orozco and Siqueiros—gave dramatic expression to strong political and social themes. Modern Mexican murals with their emotion-packed subjects and rich colors rank as some of the most famous in the world.

Andy Warhol
4 Campbell's Soup Cans
Leo Castelli Gallery

José Orozco
Zapatistas
The Museum of Modern Art, New York

Mexican Painters
José Maria Velasco 1840-1912
Saturnino Herran 1887-1918
José Clemente Orozco 1883-1949
Diego Rivera 1886-1957
David Alfaro Siqueiros 1896-1974
Rufino Tamayo 1899-1991

ORIENTAL ART

During all the years that Western Art was developing, Eastern or Oriental Art was flourishing in China, Japan, Persia and India. The style of Oriental Art is entirely different from Western Art because it developed under the influence of Buddhism and never portrayed the predominant subject matter of the West— Christianity. Oriental paintings exhibit very soft colors and delicate details. Their exquisite beauty influenced many Western artists of the 19th and 20th centuries.

18th Century Chinese
Flowers and Birds
Bibliotheque Nationale,
Paris

Chinese Painting

Chinese art showed a development of style unbroken for over 2000 years. Ideas and styles were repeated over and over again; very few motifs were ever lost. That is why it is often difficult to distinguish a very old Chinese painting from a more recent one. Some of Chinese artists' greatest achievements were the landscape paintings done on scrolls. In a scroll painting, all the details are drawn into a wide vista which stretches out like a scene one sees from a passing car. Slowly a viewer turns the scroll, uncovering one part at a time from the right to the left and looking at what is almost a moving picture. Chinese landscape painters worked with ink on silk or paper, never able to erase any mark. Scroll artists also depicted animals and human figures such as mothers tending their children in a variety of activities. Chinese paintings are dated according to the dynasty or rulers at the time they were painted. The Chinese calligraphy which appears on many scrolls usually tells the story of what is portrayed by the artist.

Japanese Painting

Travelers from China to Japan in both the 8th century and the 15th century greatly influenced Japanese artists, teaching them the style of Buddhist painting and the technique of using ink on silk. From this beginning the Japanese developed their own subjects which included battle scenes, humorous events in everyday life, and caricatures such as animals behaving as pompous human beings, etc. In the 17th century the Japanese needed imposing decorations which could be easily moved about in large castles or fortresses. A group of painters designed handsome screens, each with six panels, depicting people or scenes in intense flat colors. Even today Japanese screens decorated with paintings are some of the most beautiful screens in the world. Japanese painting is usually more simple than Chinese. It is interesting to notice how the Japanese developed the idea of blank space as part of their overall design.

Ogata Korin, Japanese painting, Edo Period
Freer Gallery of Art, Washington DC

List of Painters With Pronunciation Guide

A

Albers, Josef 1888-1976
German, worked in America
Allston, Washington 1779-1843
American
Altdorfer, Albrecht 1480-1538
German
Andrea (än-drā-∂), del Sarto
1486-1531 Italian
Angelico (an-jĕl′-ĭ-kō), Fra
1387-1455 Italian
Appel (ap′-el)), Karel 1921-2006
Dutch
Arp, Hans called Jean 1888-1966
German
Audubon, John James 1786-1851
American
Avery, Milton 1893-1965
American

B

Beardon, Romare 1914-1988
American
Bellini (bel-lē′-nē) Giovanni
c. 1430-1516 Italian
Bellows, George 1882-1925
American
Benton, Thomas Hart 1889-1975
American
Bierstadt, Albert 1830-1902
American
Bingham, George Caleb 1811-1879
American
Blake, William 1757-1827 English
Bonheur (bô-nûr′), Rosa 1822-1899
French
Bonnard (bô-nár), Pierre 1867-1947
French
Bosch (bosh), Hieronymus
1450-1516 Flemish
Botticelli (bot-i-chel-ē), Sandro
1444-1510 Italian
Boucher (bü-shā), François
1703-1770 French
Bradley, John active 1832-1847
American
Braque (bräk), Georges 1882-1963
French
Bronzino (bron-zē-nō), Agnolo
1503-1572 Italian
Bruegel (broi′-g∂l), Pieter, the Elder
1525/30-1569 Flemish
Bruegel (broi′g∂l), Jan 1568-1625
Flemish

Burchfield, Charles 1893-1967
American

C

Canaletto (kä-nä-lét-tō), Giovanni
Antonio Canal 1697-1768 Italian
Caravaggio (kar-∂-vä′-dj-yō),
Michelango Merisi da 1573-1610
Italian
Carracci (kär-rät′-chē), Annibale
1560-1609 Italian
Cassatt, Mary 1845-1926 American
worked mostly in France
Catlin, George 1796-1872
American
Cézanne (sā-zan′), Paul 1839-1906
French
Chagall (shä-gäl′), Marc 1887-1985
Russian, worked in France
Chardin (shär-d∂n′), Jean Baptiste
1699-1779 French
Chase, William Merritt 1849-1916
American
Chirico (kē′-re-ko) Georgio de
1888-1978 Italian
Church, Frederick Edwin 1826-1900
American
Claude of Lorraine 1600-1682
French, worked mostly in Italy
Cole, Thomas 1801-1848
American
Constable, John 1776-1837
English
Copley, John Singleton 1738-1815
American
Corot (k∂-rō), Camille 1796-1875
French
Correggio (k∂-rej′-yo), Antonia
Allegri 1495-1534 Italian
Courbet (kü-bā), Gustave
1819-1877 French
Cranach (krä′-nakh), Lukas the Elder
1472-1553 German
Curry, John Steuart 1897-1946
American
Cuyp (koip), Aelbert 1620-1691
Dutch

D

Dalí (dä′-lē), Salvador 1904-1989
Spanish
Daumier (dō-myā′), Honore
1808-1879 French

David (dä-vēd′), Jacques-Louis
1748-1825 French
Davis, Stuart 1894-1946 American
Degas (d∂-gä′), Edgar 1834-1917
French
De Hooch (d∂-hoex), Pieter
1629-1688 Dutch
De Kooning, Willem 1904-1997
Dutch, working in America
Delacroix (d∂-la-krwä′), Eugène
1798-1863 French
Delaunay (d∂ lō-nā′), Robert
1885-1941 French
Delaunay (d∂ lō-nā′), Sonia Terk
1885-1979 Russian active France
Derain (de-ran′), André 1880-1954
French
De Staël (de-stäl), Nicolas
1914-1955 French
Douglas, Aaron 1899-1979
American
Drouais (drü-ā), François Hubert
1727-1775 French
Dubuffet (dü-bü-fā), Jean
1901-1985 French
Duchamp (dü-shän), Marcel
1877-1968 French
Dufy (dü-fē′), Raoul, 1877-1953
French
Durand, Asher Brown
1796-1886 American
Dürer (dür′-∂r), Albrecht
1471-1528

E

Eakins, Thomas 1844-1916
American
El Greco, original name: Doménikos
Theotocopoulos 1541-1614
Greek, worked in Spain
Ensor (en′-sor), James 1860-1949
Belgium
Ernst, Max 1891-1976 German

F

Fantin-Latour (fan-tin lä-toor′), Henri
1836-1904 French
Feininger, Lyonel 1871-1956
American
Fragonard (fra-gō-när′), Jean-Honoré
1732-1806 French
Francis, John 1808-1886
American
Francis, Sam 1923-1994 American